KING ARTHUR

AND KNIGHTS

...BLE

...ultant

www.raintreepublishers.co.uk
Visit our website to find out
more information about
Raintree books.

To order:
☎ Phone +44 (0) 1865 888066
🖷 Fax +44 (0) 1865 314091
💻 Visit www.raintreepublishers.co.uk

Raintree is an imprint of Capstone Global Library Limited, a company incorporated in
England and Wales having its registered office at 7 Pilgrim Street, London, EC4V 6LB –
Registered company number: 6695582

"Raintree" is a registered trademark of Pearson Education Limited, under licence to
Capstone Global Library Limited

Text © Stone Arch Books, 2009
First published by Stone Arch Books in 2007
First published in hardback in the United Kingdom in 2009
First published in paperback in the United Kingdom in 2010
The moral rights of the proprietor have been asserted.

Art Director: Heather Kindseth
Cover Graphic Designer: Heather Kindseth and Kay Fraser
Interior Graphic Designer: Heather Kindseth

Edited in the UK by Laura Knowles
Printed and bound in China by Leo Paper Products Ltd

ISBN 978-1406212488 (hardback)
13 12 11 10 09
10 9 8 7 6 5 4 3 2 1

ISBN 978-1406213508 (paperback)
14 13 12 11 10
10 9 8 7 6 5 4 3 2 1

British Library Cataloguing in Publication Data
Hall, Margaret, 1947-
King Arthur & the knights of the Round Table. -- (Graphic revolve)
741.5-dc22
A full catalogue record for this book is available from the British Library.

TABLE OF CONTENTS

INTRODUCING...

King Arthur

Lancelot

Guinevere

MERLIN

GALAHAD

MORDRED

CHAPTER 1

Long ago, in a dark time, two mighty armies fought.

Uther Pendragon, king of Britain, fought Gorlois, the duke of Cornwall. Uther wanted to marry the duke's beautiful wife, Igraine.

I would give anything to beat my enemy.

Anything, my lord?

Uther Pendragon won the battle. Gorlois was killed, and Igraine became the new queen of Britain.

Nine months later, a child's cry is heard through the darkness.

And in the darkness, Uther's promise is remembered.

Twelve years later, Merlin left his hidden valley and travelled to the royal city of London.

It's the wizard!

Why is he here?

All the knights of the kingdom must gather here on Christmas Day!

On the chosen day . . .

Arthur was in too much of a hurry to read the words on the stone.

Arthur hurried back to his father and brother.

It's the sword from the stone!

Sir Kay knew the sword at once. He had already tried to pull it from the stone.

How did you get this, Arthur? We must return to the town square!

Kay needed a sword, Father. I remembered seeing this one. I was only going to borrow it.

Arthur soon gathered a group of knights.

They fought the rebel dukes of England and Wales who did not accept Arthur's rules.

KLANG!

Suddenly, during the battle . . .

Let all men whose hearts are full of bravery and truth hear my words.

Arthur is the true son of Uther Pendragon! As long as he rules, the kingdom shall never fall.

Merlin's words stopped the fighting.

In their hearts that day, every man crowned Arthur the true king of Britain.

CHAPTER 2

At one time, King Arthur fought Pellinore, lord of the Ghastly Forest.

KRAK!

Before Pellinore could strike the helpless Arthur, Merlin made Arthur disappear from the battle.

What is happening?

Merlin! Where am I?

Arthur got into the Lady's boat. It took him to the centre of the lake.

The boat carried Arthur back to shore. By then, the Lady of the Lake was gone.

Excalibur is mine!

Which do you like better, the sword or its scabbard?

The sword, of course!

That scabbard is worth ten swords. As long as you wear it, you cannot be wounded. Keep it safe.

Arthur and Merlin rode back the way they had come.

Soon we will pass Pellinore's kingdom.

I will fight him again! With Excalibur I can win!

Leave him alone, Arthur. He is a brave knight. In the future, he will serve you well.

25

This is the Seat Perilous. Only the world's most noble knight shall sit here. Anyone else who tries will die.

These are the duties of a knight of the Round Table.

CHAPTER 4

On one evil night . . .

Queen Guinevere has been kidnapped!

Soon, you shall be my wife. Ha ha!

The wicked Prince Melwas locked her in his fortress.

Arthur and his men rode to free their queen.

ROAAAR!

ZZAK!

I owe you my life, sir knight!

Lancelot returned Elaine to her father's castle.

Welcome. I am King Pelles. For freeing my daughter, Elaine, you shall always have my sword whenever you need it.

King Pelles celebrated Lancelot's brave rescue of Elaine.

But the king also had plans for the noble knight and his lovely daughter.

Lancelot shall soon drink the potion. The prophecy shall come true.

A witch had shown King Pelles a strange vision. Whoever would bear Lancelot's child would give birth to the greatest knight in the world.

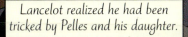

Lancelot realized he had been tricked by Pelles and his daughter.

He also knew Guinevere would be angry to hear he was wed, because she loved him.

He felt ashamed. So he rode off into a deep forest, far away from Camelot.

In good time, Elaine's son was born. She named him Galahad and raised him in a faraway castle among wise men and women.

Many years passed. Lancelot became a wild knight of the woods.

And so Lancelot returned to Camelot.

43

CHAPTER 5

Arthur's knights passed through many adventures as they searched for the Holy Grail.

Finally, three of Arthur's knights — Galahad, Percival, and Bors — came to a ruined castle.

Look! It is Lancelot.

Galahad drank from the cup, and then . . .

Galahad and the Grail were never seen again.

His fellow knights returned to Camelot without him

Arthur was right. Evil days fell upon the land. The wicked knight Mordred was plotting evil.

Mordred desired to be the king of Britain.

But first I must get rid of Arthur's best knight, Lancelot!

So the evil knight began whispering . . .

What? Lancelot and the queen are in love?

I can't believe it!

It is true. The queen must go. It is the law!

Soon the whispers reached Arthur. He had no choice but to send Guinevere away.

When Lancelot heard the news, he left Camelot as well.

Arthur was alone. And Mordred continued to plot in the shadows.

Arthur is weak. Join me, and we will rule Britain.

Mordred did his evil work well. Soon he had gathered an army.

Arthur knew a great battle was coming.

Ah, Guinevere and Lancelot. The two people I loved most are gone. And so I fight alone.

The price of battle was high.

That night, Arthur dreamed . . .

Merlin, Merlin, where are you?

It was not Merlin, but Galahad who appeared in a vision.

Do not fight this day, Arthur. Make peace with Mordred. In a month, Lancelot will come to help you.

Suddenly, Arthur awoke.

But then a snake bit one of Mordred's men.

He drew his sword to kill the snake.

AARGH!

A sword! Charge!

Both armies rushed into battle.

Arthur knew he was dying.

You must do something for me, good Sir Bors.

Anything, my king.

As you wish.

Throw Excalibur into the lake. Then tell me what you see.

Sir Bors raced to the magic lake.

I cannot throw such a fine sword away.

Bors kept the sword and returned to Arthur.

Nothing happened, my lord.

You are lying! Go back and throw the sword in the lake.

Twice Sir Bors travelled to the lake. And twice he could not bring himself to throw the sword.

Finally . . .

WHOOSH!

6

I kept my promise, didn't I, my lady?

Indeed you did, good Arthur. Now come to the island of Avalon. A friend waits for you there.

Merlin!

And so the rule of King Arthur and his Knights of the Round Table came to an end.

But legends say that he will return some day . . . when the world needs him most.

ABOUT SIR THOMAS MALORY

The story of King Arthur is an ancient legend that storytellers passed down for many generations. The story was first told sometime before the 11th century. Finally, in the 15th century, Sir Thomas Malory wrote down his version of these stories. He titled the collection *The Book of King Arthur and His Noble Knights of the Round Table*.

People know little about Malory's interest in the stories of King Arthur. He likely heard different versions of these stories when he was growing up. Perhaps his life experience as a knight helped him better understand the good and evil forces in the King Arthur stories.

ABOUT THE AUTHOR

M. C. Hall has written more than 80 fiction and non-fiction books for children, including science books, biographies, and fairy tales. She likes to read, walk on the beach, garden, and ski. She lives in Boston, USA.

ABOUT THE ILLUSTRATOR

C. E. Richards grew up reading comic books, C. S. Lewis, J. R. R. Tolkien, and watching *Star Wars*. He is a graduate of Savannah College of Art and lives in Atlanta, USA, where he is working on book and magazine illustrations, comic books, poster design, playbill illustration, and album artwork for CDs.

GLOSSARY

archbishop (arch-BISH-up) - the ruler of bishops in some Christian religions

duke (DYOOK) - in Britain, a person ranked lower than a prince

fortress (FOR-truhss) - a group of buildings protected by walls and forts

hermit (HUR-mit) - a person who lives alone and away from others

joust (JOWST) - a battle with lances or spears fought between knights on horseback

moat (MOHT) - a deep, wide ditch filled with water that surrounds a castle or fortress and keeps people away

perilous (PARE-uhl-uhss) - dangerous

potion (PO-shuhn) - a drink with special powers

prophesy (PROF-uh-see) - a prediction

rebel (REB-uhl) - a person who doesn't follow rules

scabbard (SKAB-urd) - a case that people wear to hold a sword

wizard (WIZ-urd) - a person with magical powers

BACKGROUND ON
THE KNIGHTS OF
THE ROUND TABLE

The stories of King Arthur and the Knights of the Round Table take place in Britain during the Middle Ages, a time period that lasted from the 5th to the 15th century CE. This was a period of unrest in Britain and Europe as people fought many wars for control of the land. Britain wasn't a united country at the time.

Kings and lords throughout what is now England, Wales, and Scotland ruled over small regions scattered across the countryside.

Many people wonder if the legends of King Arthur are real and if the places in the story really existed.

Some historians believe that the castle of Camelot and the island of Avalon are based on real places in England. For example, some people believe that Arthur is buried beneath the town of Glastonbury. Visitors still travel to England to retrace the steps of King Arthur and his knights.

KING ARTHUR'S BRITAIN

N

W · E

S

🏰 POSSIBLE
LOCATIONS
OF CAMELOT

SCOTLAND

ENGLAND

WALES

London •

Glastonbury
✕

*(legendary
burial site of
King Arthur)*

*English
Channel*

Atlantic Ocean

DISCUSSION QUESTIONS

1. Why did the Round Table break into two pieces?

2. At the end of the story, we find out that King Arthur and the Knights of the Round Table will return some day. Name some times when you could use the help of Arthur and the knights.

3. Would you like to go back to the times of King Arthur? Why or why not?

4. When Arthur was a boy, how did people know that he was really the king?

WRITING PROMPTS

1. Imagine that you were given the sword Excalibur. Explain what you would do with its magical powers. (Remember, the sword can only be used for good.)

2. Describe your favourite character in the story. Is it Arthur or Guinevere? Lancelot or Merlin? What does your favourite character look like? Why do you like this character the best?

3. The Knights of the Round Table go on a quest to find the Holy Grail. Their journey took a long time. Write about a quest, or journey, that you went on. What did you find at the end of it?

Black Beauty

Black Beauty, a handsome colt living in Victorian England, had a happy childhood growing up in the peaceful countryside. In his later years, he encounters terrible illness and a frightening stable fire. Things go from bad to worse when Black Beauty's new owners begin renting him out for profit. Black Beauty endures a life of mistreatment and disrespect in a world that shows little regard for the wellbeing of animals.

The Hunchback of Notre Dame

Hidden away in the bell tower of the Cathedral of Notre Dame, Quasimodo is treated like a beast. Although he is gentle and kind, he has the reputation of a frightening monster because of his physical deformities. He develops affection for Esmeralda, a gypsy girl who shows him kindness in return. When the girl is sentenced to an unfair death by hanging, Quasimodo is determined to save her. But those closest to Quasimodo have other plans for the gypsy.

Treasure Island

Jim Hawkins had no idea what he was getting into when the pirate Billy Bones showed up at the doorstep of his mother's inn. When Billy dies suddenly, Jim is left to unlock his old sea chest, which reveals money, a journal, and a treasure map. Joined by a band of honourable men, Jim sets sail on a dangerous voyage to locate the loot on a faraway island. The violent sea is only one of the dangers they face. They soon encounter a band of bloodthirsty pirates determined to make the treasure their own!

Robin Hood

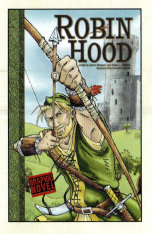

Robin Hood and his Merrie Men are the heroes of Sherwood Forest. Taking from the rich and giving to the poor, Robin Hood and his loyal followers fight for the downtrodden and oppressed. As they outwit the cruel Sheriff of Nottingham, Robin Hood and his Merrie Men are led on a series of exciting adventures.

GRAPHIC REVOLVE

If you have enjoyed this story, there are many more exciting tales for you to discover in the Graphic Revolve collection...

20,000 Leagues Under the Sea
Black Beauty
Dracula
Frankenstein
Gulliver's Travels
The Hound of the Baskervilles
The Hunchback of Notre Dame
King Arthur and the Knights of the Round Table
Robin Hood
The Strange Case of Dr Jekyll and Mr Hyde
Treasure Island
The War of the Worlds